GREAT CAREERS

FOR PEOPLE INTERESTED IN...

Art & Design

Gillian Bartlett

KOGAN PAGE EDITION EDITED BY
Joanna Grigg

KOGAN
PAGE

First published in 1993 in Canada by Trifolium Books Inc. and Weigl Educational Publishers Limited

This edition published in 1996 by Kogan Page Ltd.

Kogan Page Limited
120 Pentonville Road
London N1 9JN

© 1996, Trifolium Books Inc. and Weigl Educational Publishers Limited

British Library Cataloguing in Publication Data

A CIP record for this book is available from the British Library.

ISBN 0 7494 2079 0

Design concept: Julian Cleva
Design and layout: Warren Clark
Printed and bound in Great Britain by
Caledonian International Book Manufacturing Ltd, Glasgow

The activities in this book have been tested and are safe when carried out as suggested. The publishers can accept no responsibility for any damage caused or sustained by use or misuse of ideas or materials mentioned in the activities.

Acknowledgements
I would like to thank those people who are featured in this book for giving so generously of their time for the interviews, photography sessions and revisions of manuscript. Their dedication to their chosen careers has made our task an easy one.

Sincere thanks are also due to Elizabeth Legge, Art Curator at the University of Toronto, whose sage advice, invaluable contacts, and generous support were instrumental in the development of this volume. In addition, Tanya Biniowsky deserves thanks for her valuable suggestions and continued interest in this text, as do Rosalind Goss and Carole Wagland.

Those at Trifolium Publishing, in particular Mary Kay Winter, Diane Klim and Trudy Rising helped make this book a joy to work on. And, as always, my husband, Kenneth has been a knowledgeable and enthusiastic supporter of this project from start to finish. *GB*

Dedication
This book is dedicated to the memory of Roy Bartlett, who together with his wife, Cavell, always took pleasure from beautiful things.

Contents

Featured profiles

Careers at a glance

Jeanne Capone

Faux Finisher

PERSONAL PROFILE

Career: Faux finisher. "I think of myself as an artistic photocopier. I can see marble, a flower, wood grain — anything — and I can copy it exactly."

Interests: "Any physical activity. I love to roller blade, garden, work out at the gym, you name it. I have to be active or I go crazy."

Latest accomplishment: "I painted a mural that covered three walls in a client's dining room. It was a view of an old stone wall and some stairs leading into a garden with ivy and flowers. It turned out perfectly."

Why I do what I do?: "It's physical. And I like working with colours."

I am: "Efficient. If I'm at work, I really push myself. But if I get a job done in less time than I expected, I go and do something else. I'm not a workaholic."

What I wanted to be when I was at school: "Even when I was seven years old I knew I wanted to be an artist. I was always drawing and making things."

What a faux finisher does

"**F**aux" is a French word that means "false" or "fake". A "finisher" applies the final coat of paint to a surface. So as a faux finisher, Jeanne Capone spends her days tricking the human eye. Her job is to make things appear to be something they're not. She can take an ordinary plaster wall and make it look like it's made from brick, or wood, or even marble.

Jeanne also paints murals. She could make your dining room look like a classical Greek temple, or bedroom look like a summer garden in full bloom. You may not have the real thing, but Jeanne's job is to make you feel like you do.

Planning a finish

Often clients want Jeanne to match an existing finish. For example, they might want her to make a door frame look like it's made from the same marble that's on the floor. Others just want a decorative finish in a combination of colours. Jeanne will prepare several samples for these clients to consider. As she explains, "It's important they check the samples in all kinds of light. Sometimes the colours change under electric light, or sometimes the details seem to disappear."

Murals require more planning. "First, I do a rough pencil sketch," says Jeanne. "Then, if the clients like the general idea, I colour it in. We discuss the plan several times, and each time I do a larger scale version showing more and more of the details. The clients have to be able to see exactly what the mural will be like before I begin. You don't want to be making major changes after you start work on something like that!"

Getting the job done

Jeanne employs painters to prepare the surface for her finishing work. These painters remove any old wallpaper, fill in cracks, and apply a primer coat of paint to seal the wall. Only then will Jeanne set to work.

Once Jeanne starts a job, it goes quite quickly. "I do all the hardest

Sometimes Jeanne is asked to paint cartoon figures like this monkey which appears to be snorkelling at the bottom of a pool.

parts first," she explains, "like the picky bits in corners and around doors. Then I do the big surfaces." If the finish is simple to apply and the room is small, Jeanne can complete the job in just a few hours. On the other hand, some jobs can take several days. Jeanne may have to work on scaffolding in very high places. Even the smallest mural requires great care and precision.

"I make sure the clients see the work every day," Jeanne emphasizes. "That way I can catch problems early. It's important to give the clients exactly what they want." Jeanne's careful preparation and attention to detail have paid off for her. She always has several jobs lined up, thanks to referrals from her satisfied clients.

Jeanne can apply a faux finish to almost any surface. She treated both this coffee table and entertainment centre with a technique called "sponging". With a natural sponge, she dabs on several different coats of colour. She may use as many as seven colours to get the right effect.

All in a day's work

As a self-employed person, Jeanne Capone can afford to set her own hours. She insists on being at the job site between 9:00 a.m. and 3:00 p.m. only. That way, she gets to spend lots of time with her husband and two sons.

Be prepared

But in truth, the evenings aren't all free. In fact, much of the preparation for a job happens the night before. For one thing, Jeanne needs to mix her paints. She buys basic white acrylic or house paint and then tints it herself to get the colours just right. It takes nearly an hour to achieve the proper effect.

When this is done, Jeanne spends time preparing samples for her next client. As she observes, "The preparation is critical. For example, if I've been asked to copy a specific piece of marble, I'll practice a lot until I've figured out some tricks for doing it quickly. You can be on site for three days. Or, if you do your homework in the evenings, you can learn how to do it in a single day."

Jeanne loads her car with supplies. "Travelling is part of the job," she observes. "I drive a lot each year just going to different work sites."

On site

Once on site at 9:00 the next morning, Jeanne works intensely. This day she is producing a mural for an outside wall. She has already drawn a grid on the sample picture. Then, using a level and a long ruler, she draws a grid with the same number of squares directly on the wall. That way, she can reproduce the sample picture on the wall, matching up the details square by square.

"Some people make a slide of the sample mural and project the image right on the wall. Then they fill in the colours. But I prefer to draw a mural free hand," remarks Jeanne. "That way it's easy to make slight changes to suit the clients' requests. And I'm always adding extra details here and there.

"You have to work all over a mural," she cautions. "If you start on

Jeanne always has her supplies with her, ready to make slight colour changes.

In the eye of the beholder

"Trompe l'oeil" is a French expression which means "to fool the eye". This term is applied to works of art that are designed to make the eye think it is seeing the item itself rather than just a picture of it. Here, Jeanne has used trompe l'oeil techniques in a bathroom to make the viewer think that the green curtain is real. As Jeanne remarks, "Trompe l'oeil work combines the skill of an engineer with the eye of an artist. It has to be both technically precise and artistically pleasing."

Monday in one corner and end up on Thursday in another, it's not all going to look the same. Your brushes might get worn. Or your tints might change." Instead, Jeanne spends the day working on the background of the picture. She leaves the details in the foreground until tomorrow.

For sizeable jobs, Jeanne may employ people to help her. "I might get workers to block in simple colours for me. Or they can do jobs like drawing in the bricks for a fake brick wall."

Jeanne touches up the ivy leaves on an outdoor mural she has created to cover a garage wall.

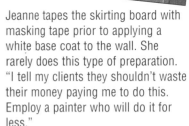

Jeanne tapes the skirting board with masking tape prior to applying a white base coat to the wall. She rarely does this type of preparation. "I tell my clients they shouldn't waste their money paying me to do this. Employ a painter who will do it for less."

Activity

Enlarge a picture

In this activity, you will use Jeanne's grid technique to enlarge a picture. You will need a picture from an old magazine, a large sheet of paper, a ruler, a pencil and paints or markers.

3. Using a pencil, practise copying the smaller picture, square by square, onto the larger paper.
4. When you have finished, use paints or markers to colour in your work.

From a small grid plan to an enormous mural — try your own hand at Jeanne's technique.

Procedure

1. Choose a small picture that appeals to you. Cut it out and, using a ruler and pencil, draw a grid over it. Space the lines evenly. Don't make the squares too large. They should be about the width of your thumb.
2. Next, take a much larger sheet of paper. Draw a grid with the same number of squares as the original, but this time make the squares three or four times as large.

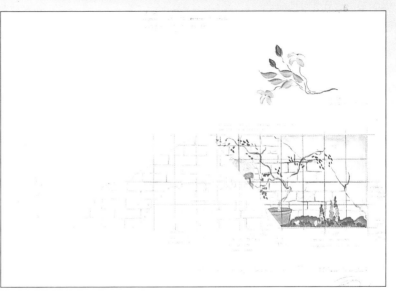

How to become a faux finisher

Jeanne's school didn't offer art courses, so after school, she took formal art classes for three years. "We did a little bit of everything," she recalls. "Life drawing, pottery, illustrations." At first, Jeanne was set on illustrating children's books. But she soon found that her interests lay in copying colour and design.

After her general art training, Jeanne worked as a waitress to earn a living. Meanwhile, she spent all her free hours practising faux finishes at home. She also painted ordinary vases to match different fabric samples. Jeanne arranged to sell her vases in expensive, up-market shops. Her designs proved popular and several customers employed her to match their own fabrics to different items like lamps and tables.

Then came Jeanne's lucky break. She applied to help restore an old

Gilding

Many faux finishers also do gilding. Gilding means covering an object with a thin layer of real gold. As Jeanne explains, "You put glue on the item. You let it dry just the right amount. Then you pick up a small, paper-thin sheet of gold and press it firmly onto the surface."

The process may sound simple, but it's tricky to get it just right. The sheets are flimsy and tend to crinkle. If the glue is too wet, the gold goes dull. If it's too dry, the gold won't stick. And it's easy to make a mistake and leave gaps. Because gold is expensive, a single error can be costly.

A plaster panel, painted and gilded by Jeanne.

theatre that was famous for its lavish decorations. "I showed the manager of the project a portfolio of my work. He was impressed. I'd worked hard to make it look professional. And it paid off."

Jeanne was employed at the theatre full time for 18 months.

"It taught me a lot about working in big spaces and with different types of plaster," she recalls. It also impressed the private clients she approached when the restoration was complete. In fact, Jeanne has produced faux finishes and murals full time ever since.

Is this career for you?

Artistic talent and an eye for colour are obviously important qualities for a faux finisher. But that's not all. If you want to be a success, you need business skills as well. "For one thing," Jeanne remarks, "you need to have a feeling for prices. You have to be able to estimate how long a job will take and what the materials will cost."

The lack of a set salary doesn't bother Jeanne. "I know how far ahead I'm booked, so I know how much money I can spend." And she relishes the freedom her job brings her. "I'm a week at one place at the *most*. And then I go to another place and meet new people," she enthuses. "You have to like people to do this. Most of the clients are great. But some people get very very picky or they can't make up their minds. You just have to have patience."

If you've stained a favourite chair, Jeanne can paint the fabric to cover the mark. Her clients asked for the flowers painted here. "You have to have confidence in yourself to work on an existing piece of furniture like this," remarks Jeanne. "You can't afford to make a mistake."

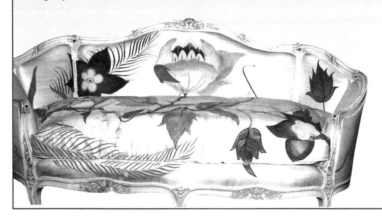

Career planning

Ask employees at a paint shop to put you in touch with a painting contractor. Ask to spend a day at work with the contractor. Make a note of how much of the day is spent doing business and how much doing painting.

In the careers department at your school, find a prospectus from an art school that teaches the techniques of faux finishing. What other art courses, including perspective and life drawing, are included in the course?

Making Career Connections

Interview an interior decorator. Find out what the latest trends are in finishing walls and furniture.

Examine the finishes used in a newly renovated building (such as a theatre, shop, restaurant or gallery). Whenever you see an unusual finish, ask the manager of the building who applied it and how it was done.

Getting started

Interested in being a faux finisher? Here's what you can do now.

1. Study art, especially life drawing, shadow drawing, illustration and design.
2. Find a paint shop that stocks kits for marbling or sponging finishes. Buy a kit and practise on a piece of furniture.
3. Study the growing habits of plants, how their leaves sit and how their blossoms are carried. Keep a notebook in which to draw your observations.
4. Get a part-time job in a building supplies shop. Find out which products work best for finishing different construction materials. Practise estimating the amount and cost of materials needed for a particular job.
5. Volunteer to work on the scenery and sets for a school play.
6. Obtain permission to design and produce a large mural for use at a fund-raising event.

Related careers

Here are some related careers you may want to look into.

Decorator
Prepares surfaces such as walls and ceilings. Applies paint, wallpaper, fabric, or other decorative coatings.

Plasterer
Finishes walls with wet plaster. Makes and installs decorative items such as mouldings, plaques and columns.

Furniture restorer
Strips and refinishes wooden furniture with stains, varnishes and lacquers.

Tiler
Installs ceramic, marble and other durable finishes to floors and walls.

Stone mason
Chisels, carves and sets blocks of marble or stone for staircases, entrances and walls.

Scenery painter
Paints stage sets, props and scenery.

Futurewatch

Unusual and unique interiors are becoming very popular. Wealthy people who have the desire to produce something beautiful are often prepared to spend thousands of pounds just to paper a single room. "But I can paint a mural for a quarter of that," explains Jeanne. "There are no seams showing, and I can vary colours to compensate for shadows." For those with less money, marbling and sponging are affordable options. That means faux finishing has a great future. "No question about it."

Sergio Mourguet

Jeweller

PERSONAL PROFILE

Career: Jeweller. "When people come back years later to tell me how much they love the jewellery I made for them — that's a fantastic feeling."

Interests: "I spend time at my cottage. I go canoeing there. And I also enjoy riding my mountain bike through the woods."

Latest accomplishment: "I designed some key chains and bottle openers for use in a TV advertisement. I was under pressure because the advertisers needed the pieces really fast."

Why I do what I do: "I love to do things with my hands."

I am: "Very happy at my work."

What I wanted to be when I was at school: "I never had my mind set on anything special. I think I always had the idea that whatever I chose, I knew I would be content."

What a jeweller does

As owner of his own jewellery shop, Sergio Mourguet is involved in all aspects of producing jewellery. He explains with satisfaction, "I design the jewellery. I make it. I sell it. And I service it afterwards if it needs attention."

Designing ideas

To attract customers, Sergio keeps a large stock of interesting necklaces, earrings, chains, and other pieces on display. Since he opened his shop ten years ago, Sergio estimates he has designed well over 1000 different items.

Sometimes Sergio comes up with the ideas himself. At other times, the customers explain what they want.

"If people come in with an idea I don't think will work, usually I can coax them to change their minds," explains Sergio. "I want to make sure they will be happy with the piece."

The real thing

Once a design is decided, it needs to be turned into reality. This process can be time-consuming. It takes Sergio about three hours from start to finish to create a simple ring. More complicated pieces take longer.

But once the first piece is made, Sergio can duplicate it easily. To do this, he makes rubber moulds that he can use time and again to make copies. Of course, for special items,

Sergio will "break the mould". That way customers know the piece is unique. There isn't another one like it in the world.

It's a Fact

Not all gold jewellery is pure yellow in colour. If a jeweller mixes gold with copper, the final product will have a pink tinge. Adding nickel makes gold look white. And adding a combination of copper, silver and zinc gives a green effect to the metal.

Techniques of the trade

Forging

In forging, metal is hammered into different, thinner shapes. The hammer blows cause distortion of the metallic crystals. If the crystals are too closely packed, the metal will become brittle and crack. To prevent this, jewellers "anneal" or heat the metal. This loosens the crystals and the metal becomes more flexible again.

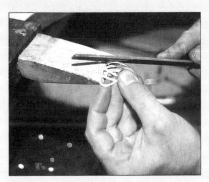

Smoothing the edges of a forged brooch.

Carving a wax ring to cast a gold ring.

Casting

In casting, melted metal is poured into a mould. Jewellers often make plaster moulds using the "lost wax" technique. This involves carving a wax version of the object they want, such as a ring or pin. The wax shape is coated in plaster and baked at a very high heat. The wax melts and burns off. This leaves an empty space inside the plaster that is in the desired shape, ready to be filled with liquid silver or gold.

Fusing and soldering

Jewellers use torches to join pieces of metal together such as the links on a chain. In fusing, the two pieces are melted slightly so their edges blend and they will stick together. In soldering, a tiny amount of another metal is heated and melted at the join. Once the metal cools and hardens, it holds the pieces together.

Fusing the band on a ring that was cut down in size.

All in a day's work

"I leave home at 8.30 every day," reports Sergio. "But I don't open the shop until 10.00. That gives me time to do the outside work like banking and going to my suppliers."

Sergio has many places to visit. He may need to pick up oxygen and propane for his torch. Jeweller's wax, "rouge" for polishing and base metals like copper and nickel come from another supplier. Gold and silver, in thin wafers, are purchased from bankers. "And some days I pick up orders from the engraver or the diamond setter," Sergio comments.

At the bench

Once he opens the store, Sergio goes to his bench, carrying a cup of hot coffee. "Every day I have my coffee and organize my bench. That's a rule," he says firmly. "I clean everything because it's very easy to get messy. And when I'm doing 20 different things I have to be very well organized."

First, Sergio turns to the special orders from customers. He checks to make sure that all the items he has promised for that day are ready. Then he starts on new orders. Perhaps he is working on a commissioned necklace that needs careful hammering into shape. Or he could be designing a new pair of cufflinks. These jobs are the most challenging and take the most energy.

Sergio keeps an eye out for customers as he sits working at his

Sergio at work at his bench. How many different tools can you identify in this picture?

Sergio discusses a new ring with a customer. On the counter is a set of ring sizes used to measure the size of a customer's finger.

Brooches like these are always big sellers. They make perfect gifts.

When is gold not gold?

The purest gold is 24 carat gold (24ct). That means it is 100 percent gold. No other metal has been mixed with it.

But jewellers don't use pure gold very often, because it is very soft and very expensive. Instead, they use alloys: they mix pure gold with less costly metals.

Mark on Jewellery	Ratio of gold to other metal	Percent pure gold
24ct	24 parts gold: 0 parts other metal	100
18ct	18 parts gold: 6 parts other metal	75
14ct	14 parts gold: 10 parts other metal	58.5
10ct	10 parts gold: 14 parts other metal	41.6

bench. They will browse through the display cases on the ground level or climb up the few steps to where he is working at the back of the shop.

"Maybe 12 or 15 people walk into the shop each day. But I have an average of ten sales a day, which is a high percentage," says Sergio happily.

Sometimes customers have small repairs to be done. "I try to do the repairs right away," explains Sergio. "It's easier for me to keep organized,

and also they don't have to wait. Everybody always wants everything fast. But it is also true that I work better under pressure. I think sometimes I wait until the last minute myself because I do better work then."

Production

After 6:00 or so in the evening, Sergio closes his shop doors. But it's not time to go home yet. This is when he does the mass production of

the pieces for his display cases. Sergio takes some of the hundreds of rubber moulds he has made and fills them with liquid metal. "If I'm doing ten bracelets at once," he smiles, "I find it very relaxing. When I'm doing production, it's almost as though I don't need to think."

Sometimes Sergio works until midnight. But he can't oversleep the next morning. Business is business. The shop must be open at 10.00 the next day for his customers.

Activity

Design your own ornament
The following activity gives you practice at working with metals.

You will need
- thin gloves (for protection)
- the lid from a tin of soup
- a hammer with a rounded head
- a hardwood board for hammering on
- a ruler and pencil
- metal cutters or strong scissors
- thin copper wire

Procedure
1. Place the lid on the board and hammer it all over, on both sides, until it is perfectly flat.
2. With a pencil and ruler, divide the lid into eight equal sections.

WARNING!
The cut edges are very sharp. Handle them with extra care. Wear rubber gloves to make sure you don't cut yourself.

Use a pencil to draw in the dotted dividing lines. Cut out each section along the solid lines

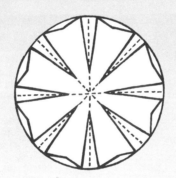

3. With the metal cutters or scissors, cut out the star shown here, or any pattern of your choice. Working on the back of the metal, lightly hammer the edges flat.

4. Loop copper wire loosely around the pencil several times. Leave a straight piece at one end that is about the length of your index finger.
5. Remove the wire from the pencil and twist the loops into an abstract design. Wind the straight piece of wire firmly around the middle of the tin star so that the loops are in the centre.
6. You can hook a safety pin onto the wire at the back to turn the star into a brooch. Or you can make several stars and string them into a mobile.

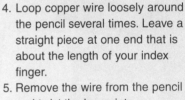

The finished tin decoration

How to become a jeweller

Sergio never expected to be a jeweller. In fact, after he finished school, he studied sociology. "When I came to this country, my brother was working for a jeweller. Since I spoke only Spanish and had to eat, it seemed a good idea to join him."

At first Sergio started with the less-skilled jobs. He cut and polished stones. And he helped to mass-produce jewellery using rubber moulds. But soon Sergio was designing his own creations. He found he had a real knack for making jewellery. After two years, he was ready to go out on his own.

While many jewellers learn on the job, this is not the only way to enter the profession. There are various training courses available. They feature courses in design, jewellers' techniques, and gemmology (the study of gems such as rubies and emeralds).

Sergio is the first to admit that his methods are sometimes unusual, compared with those taught in the colleges. "But that's partly what makes my items different," he points out. "If you go to a college there is always the danger you will learn certain patterns. Then it can be hard to break away and work in your own style."

Carats and carats

The word carat has two slightly different meanings. In one sense it tells how much gold there is in proportion to another metal. In relation to gemstones, though, it is a measure of mass, telling how heavy a diamond or emerald is.

One world-famous diamond belongs to the British crown jewels. The Great Star of Africa, as it is called, weighs 530 carats. Given that there are 5 carats in a gram, or 142 carats in an ounce, how heavy is this stone? (Answer is on page 48.)

Is this career for you?

Are you good with your hands? Do you have patience and artistic flair? If so, you might consider becoming a jeweller.

Jewels may seem glamorous. But the truth is, making jewellery can be a very messy process. You have to be prepared to get your hands dirty. And even with a good ventilation system, a jeweller must cope with noise and dust from polishing stones and with fumes from baking moulds.

Some jewellers work in large factories. But very often they are like Sergio, working alone or with a partner. Because jewels are valuable, theft is a constant worry and insurance rates are high. Sergio has been robbed but luckily never faced any danger. The thieves sneaked jewellery out of his display cabinets while he was helping some customers. Amazingly, Sergio got the stolen items back. "I try to forget about this," he says with a laugh. Still, the worry is always there.

Independent jewellers need business skills. "There's a lot of money and paper work involved in a business like this," remarks Sergio. "The banking alone has to be done two or three times a week."

Sergio's success has a price. "I get out to the country only a few times each summer, which is a shame," he laments. "Everything else is work." But then the twinkle returns to his eye. "I don't mind. These are beautiful objects. And they give people pleasure. I am very happy."

Career planning

Making Career Connections

Ask a salesperson for the names and addresses of companies that manufacture the jewellery sold at a local department store. Write to these companies and ask what training and qualifications they require when recruiting jewellers.

Ask your librarian to help you find the address of a jewellery or gemmology association. Write to the association and ask for information about training as a jeweller.

Ask your school careers adviser to help you locate colleges where jewellery arts are taught. Write and ask for copies of the course descriptions.

Visit a jeweller who works in your area. Ask permission to spend a day observing the jeweller at work. Note what styles are currently in fashion. Ask if any local jewellers take on apprentices.

Getting started

Interested in being a jeweller? Here's what you can do now.

1. Study jewellery catalogues to learn the words associated with the trade.
2. Read the stock market listings in a newspaper to determine current prices for gold and silver. Keep a chart for several weeks to record any changes in price.
3. Visit craft shows and talk to the jewellers, blacksmiths and goldsmiths there.
4. Study art, design and technology. Search out classes in sculpting, clay modelling and metal working.
5. Visit museums to study jewellery made in the past. Sketch the pieces that appeal to you.
6. Practise making things with your hands. Carve wood or wax, plasticine or ice. Train yourself to turn drawings on paper into three-dimensional objects.

Related careers

Here are some related careers you may want to look into.

Engraver
Carves or cuts patterns into metal surfaces. Works with designs (such as curlicues on silver trays) and lettering (inscribing gifts with important names or dates).

Gemmologist
Identifies and classifies real and artificial gems according to such features as clarity, colour and size. Appraises the value of jewellery items for insurance purposes.

Sculptor
Creates three-dimensional art. Fashions metal, stone, plaster and other materials into decorative objects.

Blacksmith
Fashions and welds iron into banisters, gates, grills and decorative items.

Ceramist
Makes jugs, plates, dinnerware and decorative items from clay.

Futurewatch

Humans, in all times and in all countries, have always had the urge to decorate themselves. Today, it is jewellers like Sergio who make the most long-lasting decorations. A piece of jewellery is a very personal item. As Sergio comments, "It makes a big difference to people when they know the person who has made their jewellery, even if it's not one-of-a-kind." For that reason, there will always be an emphasis on hand-made products. And, consequently, there will always be a demand for jewellers.

Sherry Phillips

Conservator

PERSONAL PROFILE

Career: Conservator. "My job is to preserve works of art."

Interests: "I enjoy outdoor activities: gardening, walking my dog, camping and canoeing. I spend a lot of time working on our 100-year-old house. But I also love curling up with a good book."

Latest accomplishment: "My gallery lent a valuable picture to a museum in Jerusalem and I brought it back to the gallery. The security at both air terminals was excellent."

Why I do what I do: "The preservation of art is important to me. It's the preservation of part of our history."

I am: "Very flexible. You have to be a problem-solver in this job."

What I wanted to be when I was at school: "I wanted to work with elderly people. I think psychology was on my mind at one point and microbiology and scientific illustration."

What a conservator does

Some conservators run their own private businesses. Others work for museums. And still others, like Sherry Phillips, are employed by art galleries. But whether they work for themselves or for an institution, conservators examine, preserve, and restore works of art.

It's not an easy task. One problem is that "art" can mean so many different things. "You can find yourself working on some pretty weird items," Sherry laughs. "But basically you specialize in paintings, or paper, or objects. 'Objects' are such things as sculpture or ceramics, or items as different as clothing, musical instruments, or even animal bones."

Keeping a watchful eye

Sherry works mostly with paintings. One of her jobs is to keep a watchful eye on conditions in the art gallery display areas. Temperature, humidity, and light levels are checked constantly. "It's rare," remarks Sherry, "but if something goes drastically wrong with the levels, we have to remove art from the display space until the problem is fixed."

When art is lent to another gallery, Sherry is asked to prepare a report on its condition. To do this, she examines the work carefully using a bright light. "I first check the condition of the frame to see if it's secure. Then I look for damage to the painting, such as scratches or scuffs," says Sherry. Her report is sent along with the painting and is used to make sure that no damage was caused in transit.

Cleaning carefully

Most of Sherry's time is spent cleaning and repairing paintings. The pictures on display are usually in top condition. On the other hand, many of the works in the gallery's storage vaults need attention, like a thorough cleaning. As Sherry explains, "Some artists apply a final coat of varnish on their paintings. But over 40 or 50 years, the varnish can become dark. Dirt from smoke and other pollution can also build up on the surface. It's my job to find the right solvents to remove these layers without harming the painting itself."

Sherry checks the readings on a "hydrothermograph". This instrument measures humidity and temperature levels. Extreme variations in moisture or temperature over a long period of time can cause cracks in paintings or wood.

Cleaning a painting requires intense concentration. "You have to watch very carefully how the paint is reacting to the chemicals you are using," cautions Sherry. "I'm currently working on a picture in which the red paints are very sensitive. So when I notice even a hint of red paint on my swab, I stop immediately."

Making paint

Until paint was sold commercially, artists mixed their own paints using natural products. The first step was to obtain the right pigment, or colour. A reddish brown pigment was made from red clay, dark brown pigment from the ink sacs of squid and scarlet by crushing the bodies of certain insects. Bright blue came from grinding a mineral called lapis lazuli into a fine powder.

Next, artists mixed their pigments with "binders". Binders help pigments stick to a surface, while also protecting them from wear and fading. For centuries, the most common binders used were egg (to make tempera paints) and walnut or linseed oil (for oil paints). But artists also used binders like sour milk and plant gums. The natural binders are still used today. In addition, modern manufacturers use synthetic binders to make acrylic and alkyd paints.

All in a day's work

Sherry arrives early at the large, bright studios where the gallery conservators work. Sometimes the shipping department will ask her to make a quick report on the condition of a painting. Or she might be asked to give advice about framing or storing a work. Often she attends meetings with other gallery staff about future exhibitions. Otherwise, it's up to Sherry what tasks she will turn to for the day.

"I try to keep several projects going at once," Sherry remarks. "Right now I'm in the middle of two, and there's a third one in a cupboard waiting to go. But I'm thinking about it all the time."

Advance planning

In fact, each project requires a great deal of advance planning. "Before I do anything," notes Sherry, "I study the work and its background. I make a file that includes photographs as well as details about the artist, the painting, and its present condition."

Almost always, the painting needs to be cleaned. It's not easy to predict how the paints in an old picture will react. So Sherry spends many hours testing different chemicals on the edges of the painting to see which work best.

Sometimes paint is flaking off, and Sherry can't tell why this is happening just from looking at the surface. "In these cases I may do an X-ray," she explains. "Sometimes I find another painting underneath. The top layer of paint might not have bonded with the first layer."

Sherry has partly finished cleaning this 200-year-old painting. "Because budgets are so tight these days," laments Sherry, "we only have time to work on paintings that are needed for exhibition. Other pieces in the vault just have to wait."

Often, Sherry finds weaknesses in the canvas. If there are tears or punctures, the painting may need to be re-lined. In this process, a new piece of canvas is bonded to the back of the old canvas.

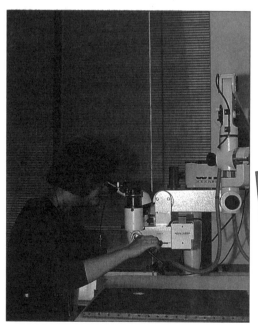

"Normal eyesight isn't good enough for working on some paintings," says Sherry. "This surgical microscope is just wonderful. The double lenses allow two people to observe at the same time. And I can attach a camera and take detailed pictures."

Sherry uses an extractor (also called an "elephant trunk") to draw off fumes as she cleans a painting.

After Sherry has completed her study, she writes a "treatment proposal". This document outlines step by step what she intends to do to the painting. Other gallery staff members discuss and approve the procedure. Only then will the treatment begin.

Picture perfect

On most days, Sherry spends several hours cleaning. She works methodically. "When you clean a painting, you always follow the lines of the image," she demonstrates. "That way, if there's a problem removing the varnish, then you're not going to see straight lines all over."

If there are bare patches, Sherry adds new paint. She makes sure her "in-painting", as it is called, will not be confused with the original work. "With in-painting, we get the colours as close to those of the surrounding paint as possible. But we won't cover any of the original paint."

For in-painting, Sherry uses a totally different paint that won't bond with the kind the artist used. For an oil painting, for example, she starts with a base coat of watercolour.

After the base coat, Sherry adds a varnish layer to isolate the area. She then paints in the finer details using an acrylic-based paint.

By the end of the day, Sherry may have worked on several paintings, all at different stages of treatment. Before heading home, she records in a file exactly what she has done to each work. Sometimes she even photographs a work to record her progress. The day has been tiring, but satisfying. And the paintings will be waiting there for her tomorrow.

How to become a conservator

Not so long ago, all conservators got their training on the job. But nowadays there are courses for those who choose this profession. Students can start some of these courses right from school. However, the entrance requirements of most courses, such as the one Sherry completed, include more education.

"To be conservators, we have to know about science as well as art," explains Sherry. "I gained a degree in science, so I had a basic knowledge of chemistry and physics. But I hadn't studied art since school. So before I was accepted onto the course, I studied art for a year. I actually painted with oils and acrylic paints, as well as studying art history."

Sherry's conservator course lasted two full years. "We learned a lot about chemicals and paints," recalls Sherry, "and how they react with each other. We also had to learn about how light affects a work of art." There were many other options, including photography and film developing.

After Sherry graduated, she could only get contract work at first. But then her lucky break came. A conservator she had worked with one summer gave Sherry a call. A full-time administrative job, as a registrar, was available in the gallery (see Related Careers). This job gave Sherry a foot in the door. And when a conservator vacancy came along, she was given the job straight away.

Most conservator courses require students to get hands-on experience before they can graduate. Kirsten Hancox spent several months working in Sherry's department. Here she sews a protective backing on an Inuit wall hanging.

Is this career for you?

"You should be an all-rounder to do this job," cautions Sherry, "because you have to enjoy both the arts and the sciences." In fact, it helps to be inquisitive and curious about everything. As Sherry comments, "Every conservator has to be a bit of a detective."

Conservators also need to be cautious. Sherry works regularly with many different chemicals. "I'm very careful when I work with chemicals," she says seriously. "I often use gloves and masks, even when I'm working with a fume hood. I want to live a long time."

Even more importantly, a conservator has to have enormous patience. "Cleaning a work of art is a painstaking process. You have to go over it inch by inch. And if you have a tight deadline for an exhibition, you have to be prepared to work through a microscope for hours at a stretch."

Art displayed out-of-doors poses special conservation problems. Here, art curator Elizabeth Legge checks James Gillespie's Sitelines for signs of damage caused by severe weather or vandals.

All this time spent on one work of art can have an emotional impact. "I do get quite possessive," grins Sherry. "I come to know every brush stroke of a work of art and can become very attached to it."

Career planning

Find out who is responsible for maintaining local works of art. Interview this person about the problems of protecting public art.

From your careers officer or local museum curator, obtain a list of institutions that offer art conservation courses. Write to one of them for information about courses and entrance requirements.

Making Career Connections

Contact a representative of the art gallery nearest you to find out how the gallery conserves its art works. If possible, arrange a tour of the conservation facilities.

Use the Yellow Pages to find the name of an art dealer. Visit the shop or gallery and ask the dealer how the artworks are protected. Discuss the effects of smoke, light, extreme temperatures and accidental damage.

Getting started

Interested in being a conservator? Here's what you can do now.
1. Study sciences, especially chemistry and physics at school.
2. Take art classes. Learn the differences between various paints such as oil, acrylic and tempera. Try your hand at wood carving or pottery.
3. Read books about art and art history.
4. Practise taking photographs. Better still, take a photography course to learn about design, focus, film speed and light exposure.
5. Volunteer to work at an art gallery in your area. Pay attention to how the objects are displayed: consider the distance between them and how they are protected. Notice the light and atmospheric conditions. What are the sources of light? How humid is the air?

Related careers

Here are some related careers you may want to look into.
Crating technician
Expert carpenter with good maths skills. Packs works of art for safe shipping.
Archaeologist
Studies the remains of older societies. Digs to uncover the foundations of early settlements. Uses findings such as broken pots or tools to suggest what life was like in vanished societies.
Security guard
Patrols gallery showrooms to ensure that visitors do not damage or steal works of art.
Registrar
Maintains the records about the works of art in a collection. Records the donors, purchase dates, etc.
Paint chemist
Works in a laboratory to develop new paints. Experiments with pigments, binders and additives.

Future watch

Unusual and unique interiors are becoming very popular. There is a definite need for more conservation. Many works of art displayed in galleries, businesses, and private homes are in need of attention. But conservation is still considered a luxury. A painting may have yellowed varnish or a tear that needs fixing. A sculpture may have a chip or need a good cleaning. But if they haven't got the money, owners will display their works of art just as they are. Therefore conservators' jobs and incomes will continue to depend on how much money is available for this service.

Johnny Gibson

Commercial Artist

PERSONAL PROFILE

Career: Commercial artist. "I pay attention to what customers want. I produce art for myself, but I also make art that people ask for and will buy."

Interests: "I've just more or less made a career from my personal interests. But I do like being outdoors. I also read quite a lot."

Latest accomplishment: "I landed a contract for developing CD-ROMS. I've hired a whole team to help. I work on the visuals."

Why I do what I do: "I enjoy it. I never went out and did things when I was younger like going to parties. I just stayed at home and painted. One year I did over a hundred different pictures."

I am: "Excited by new ideas and techniques. I'm happiest when I'm experimenting with new approaches to my work."

What I wanted to be when I was at school: "Everything. A detective one week and a nuclear physicist the next. But by the time I was 15, I knew I wanted to be an artist."

What a commercial artist does

Commercial artists are artists for hire. Many commercial artists work for large companies, such as film studios and manufacturers of greeting cards. These companies employ whole teams of artists full-time to create their products. Often, a single image is the work of several people.

Other commercial artists earn their living by freelancing. This is the case for Johnny Gibson, who works from his own studio. Sometimes Johnny is "commissioned" to complete a specific job, such as designing a poster for a play. At other times, he creates a work on his own, then offers it for sale, perhaps for use on a calendar.

But whatever the work, Johnny is his own boss. He relishes the artistic freedom.

As he says with a grin, "I've been hired and fired so many times in my life that I know what it's like to have a boss. But I don't like doing just one thing, and I like to learn how to do things by myself."

Art in print

Johnny's art has appeared in a whole range of publications. "I've done book illustration," he reports. "An author will come to me with an idea for a children's book, for example. We'll discuss the project quite a few times. Then, depending on what the author wants, I try to bring out the author's creativity with my pictures."

Like many commercial artists, Johnny also produces work for magazines. "I've done covers and I've illustrated articles," he says modestly. In fact, Johnny is also co-publisher and art director for a magazine that comes out four times a year. In his role as art director, he is responsible for the entire look of the magazine.

Versatility pays

Above all, Johnny is versatile. He's eager to take on all artistic challenges. He feels just as much at home using a computer with a mouse as he does using a paint brush or pencil. He has also moved beyond visual art to working with musical groups. He has helped them record their music, designed and produced the CD packages and marketed the recordings in shops. One of these groups was nominated for a music award.

As Johnny says, "I like to do everything." Working as a freelance commercial artist means he can make these opportunities happen.

Johnny first created these images using acrylic paints on canvas. Then, he photographed the paintings and had the film "digitized" (translated into information on a computer disk).

Johnny had to hire and train staff to help him in his latest project. The company, known as SAGO Design, is a family business. His brothers Chester and Donald, who are both school teachers, are key members on the team.

All in a day's work

Johnny's working days are long. "I get up early and start around nine or so," he reports. "And I usually work through the day, at least 14 to 16 hours." But the pace is relaxed. There is no sign of frantic tension as his staff members wander in and go quietly about their work.

"There are people here right around the clock," Johnny smiles. "Sometimes people come in here at 11 o'clock at night and start programming. They leave when they're tired, and then someone else will decide to come in at 2 or 3 o'clock and start to work. It's a fluid environment. There are no 9-to-5 days."

The digital difference

Johnny spends his mornings working on the computer. Part of that time he trains his staff and organizes their tasks. The rest of the time, Johnny works on his own images.

Today's computer programs allow artists to experiment widely with their work. After bringing an image into the computer, Johnny can manipulate it in many different ways. He can change its size, reverse it and adjust the colours. He can even change the texture to look like watercolours or crayons. He can lighten dark areas or change the surface from shiny to matte — with the click of a mouse.

Johnny works on a software design with his brother, Chester. It is for an interactive CD-ROM teaching comparative culture, language and history.

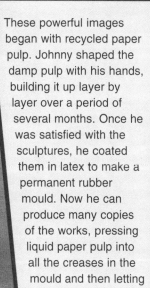

These powerful images began with recycled paper pulp. Johnny shaped the damp pulp with his hands, building it up layer by layer over a period of several months. Once he was satisfied with the sculptures, he coated them in latex to make a permanent rubber mould. Now he can produce many copies of the works, pressing liquid paper pulp into all the creases in the mould and then letting it dry. The warrior and the cougars pictured here have been given a primer coat of white. Johnny can now enhance them with coloured paints.

Original art

Johnny spends many afternoons creating new images. "I normally have three or four paintings going at once," he explains, "at various stages of completion. Some of them take up to a year, depending on the type of research that I'm doing."

Indeed, research is an important part of his work. "I try to integrate spirituality with my work," says Johnny. "So I need to do research to understand the images and the meanings behind them."

Johnny's work has many aspects: research, painting, framing his paintings and checking magazine pages before they are printed. To keep his business running smoothly, he speaks to his clients on the telephone and attends to paperwork. His days are remarkably full, but varied. And, as he says with satisfaction, "That's the way I like it."

Johnny examines prints of his painting, *Whispering Weeds*. "I don't really make money from the original picture," he explains. "Instead I make prints for posters or calendars. Often publishers want to use the art, so I sell the rights for reproduction."

This painting was one of a series of 20 lifestyle portraits. "I included symbols with each portrait," Johnny comments. In this picture, the jaguar, the owl and the moon are all symbols.

Activity

Try your hand at illustration

You have probably heard the saying, "a picture is worth a thousand words." Well, here's your opportunity to prove it.

When commercial artists are given a book or short story to illustrate, they need to read the manuscript carefully. It won't do to draw a tall, red-haired character when the text says distinctly that the character is short and has brown hair.

Choose a short story or novel that you are already familiar with. Re-read the piece, keeping an eye out for clues about how characters look. Also watch for details of the setting. If it's a room, what size is it, how is it decorated, what furniture and objects are present? If it's an outdoor scene, what is the weather like, are there any buildings, what kind of plants are growing?

Once you have re-read the story, choose a critical moment to illustrate. Plan your work with several rough sketches. Play with the location of people and objects. Use your imagination to add details not mentioned by the author but that you think would fit in. If necessary, look through books or magazines in the library to find pictures of appropriate furniture styles, costumes, or landscapes to use as models.

Then bring the critical moment in the story to life. Produce your picture with pencils, crayons, markers, paints — any materials with which you feel comfortable. When you are finished, ask a friend to read the story. Can your friend tell just what moment you have illustrated?

How to become a commercial artist

"I was always creating and inventing things, even when I was little," reports Johnny. But the year he turned 16, he realized he wanted to earn his living as an artist. He found he preferred to stay at home every weekend painting pictures, rather than going out with his friends.

Once he knew what he wanted to do in life, Johnny gathered his best paintings together in a portfolio. He showed them to tutors at a nearby college and they accepted him onto an art course immediately. Even though he was younger than most applicants, the teachers recognized that Johnny had a remarkable talent.

While he was at college, Johnny took a foundation course. "It gave me a good understanding of all the different techniques available to an artist. I learned how to work with different media like oils and acrylics.

Johnny spends time on the phone making contacts. He also attends writers' conferences. "I keep in touch, to find out about what people are working on now."

I learned the principles behind designing a picture. I even learned to work in three dimensions, in sculpture."

If Johnny had wanted to work full time in a studio, he would have applied for a job at an advertising agency or publisher. But he found he much preferred the freedom of freelancing. It took knocking on doors, contacting agencies by phone, and showing his portfolio, but he was soon working steadily on many contract jobs.

Is this career for you?

Freelancers like Johnny are never sure of what work lies ahead. This means they must be persistent in drumming up work and self-disciplined in completing it. Nobody wants to employ someone who constantly fails to meet deadlines.

But clients are also always looking for something new. So freelancers can't become discouraged if a client stops using their work for a while. As Johnny says calmly, "If you've done good work for them in the past, they'll get around to using you again."

Freelancers also need good business skills. Keeping the accounts can be tricky when there are many different projects on the go. Tracking costs and hours for different jobs takes an organized mind.

No room for ego

Creative artists working in studios face different challenges. For one thing, these artists need to be good

As an independent businessman, Jonny can choose where he works. Here he poses with his SAGO Design team by the abandoned barn near his studio. "Out here the sound is crystal clear. You can hear a pin drop. It really helps my concentration. It's wonderfully peaceful."

team players. Several different artists may work on a design as it goes through the stages of development. It can be difficult to never see a work through, from start to finish. But it's important not to feel hurt or angry about changes that are made.

A commercial artist, whether in a studio or working freelance, cannot afford to let personal ego get in the way. A commercial artist's responsibility is to create a product that suits the client. The most successful are artists like Johnny, who produce work that is consistently popular with customers. There is tremendous satisfaction from knowing people appreciate your work well enough to buy it.

Career planning

Look in the Yellow Pages under "Publishing" or "Desktop Publishing" to find agencies or companies that employ commercial artists full time. Telephone the personnel departments of these companies. Ask what qualifications are required for employment.

Choose a favourite magazine. Look for the "masthead" — the column that lists the names of the publisher, editors, managers, etc. Write a letter to the art director to say how much you enjoy the magazine. Then ask how pictures are chosen for the magazine.

Making Career Connections

In your school careers office, find course details for two or three art colleges. Read them to find out about entrance requirements and courses offered.

Ask your teacher to help you arrange a visit to a commercial art studio. "Job shadow" one of the artists for a day.

Getting started

Interested in being a commercial artist? Here's what you can do now.
1. Take all the art classes you can.
2. Produce art at school. Make posters for upcoming events, or scenery for a play.
3. Enter your pictures in a competition.
4. Make your own greeting cards. Send these original creations to family and friends.
5. Design you own calendar with a different picture for each month. Have it photocopied and bound, and give copies as gifts.
6. Work with graphics programs on a computer.
7. Develop your own portfolio. Store your finished works carefully. Mark them on the back with the date, your name, and the title.
8. Train your eye. Examine magazine illustrations. Copy those that really appeal to you. Analyse what makes them so good.

Related careers

Here are some related careers you may want to look into.
Animator
Draws figures of humans and animals in motion. Produces animated films for teaching, entertainment and marketing.
Portrait artist
Paints or draws people's pictures, usually by commission. May work anywhere, from a local fair to a formal art studio.
Desktop publisher
Responsible for the layout and design of newsletters, catalogues, reports and business forms.
Cartoonist
Creates comic strips, caricatures, and/or editorial cartoons for company newsletters, greeting cards, advertisements and signs.
Window dresser
Creates displays in store windows to attract attention and enhance the products for sale.

Futurewatch

The future for commercial artists lies in computers. Johnny has an office in a large city, a two-hour drive from his home and studio. But the locations are just micro-seconds apart on the information highway. Working from his studio, Johnny dials the computer in his city office, sending material electronically over the wires. Using the Internet address at the city office, he communicates with clients across the country. There will always be jobs for commercial artists, especially those like Johnny who keep in touch with the latest changes in technology.

Arlene Hofstader

Architect

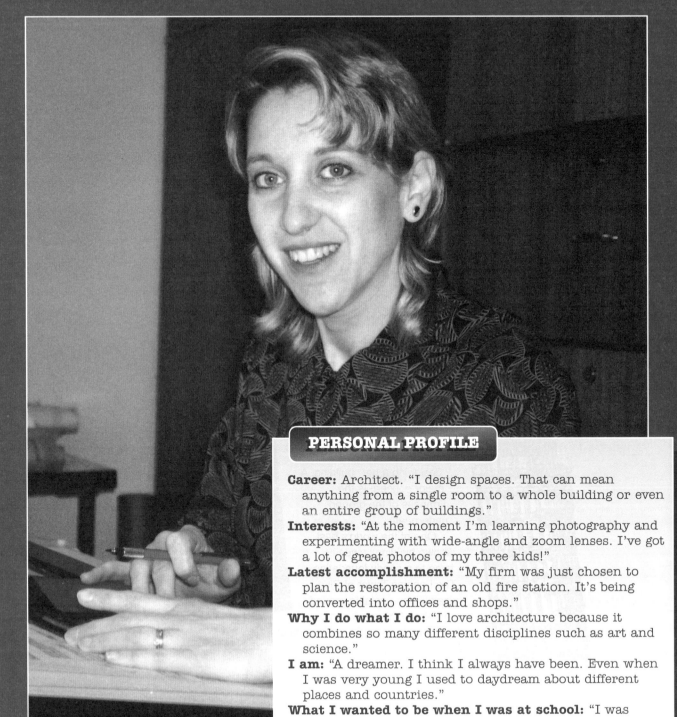

PERSONAL PROFILE

Career: Architect. "I design spaces. That can mean anything from a single room to a whole building or even an entire group of buildings."

Interests: "At the moment I'm learning photography and experimenting with wide-angle and zoom lenses. I've got a lot of great photos of my three kids!"

Latest accomplishment: "My firm was just chosen to plan the restoration of an old fire station. It's being converted into offices and shops."

Why I do what I do: "I love architecture because it combines so many different disciplines such as art and science."

I am: "A dreamer. I think I always have been. Even when I was very young I used to daydream about different places and countries."

What I wanted to be when I was at school: "I was always doodling and drawing. I thought it would be great to write about art. But as I grew older I decided that architecture was a more practical choice."

What an architect does

To understand what architects do, just think of a room you really like. Then ask yourself why. How large is this room? How high are the ceilings? How are the windows and doors arranged? How is it heated and lit? Where are the electrical switches and sockets? All of these are questions that concern architects. For, as Arlene Hofstader explains, "an architect designs and creates spaces."

Planning

Whether the job involves building a new space or renovating an old one, Arlene needs to do a lot of preparation before the hammering and sawing can begin.

"First, I interview the clients to get an idea of what they want from the space. For a house extension, for example, I ask them to describe their daily lives. Where do they spend most of their time at home? Do they like large rooms to gather in? Or do they want a group of smaller, separate rooms?"

The next step is to draw plans for the project. Arlene uses all of her technical knowledge to make sure the space will work properly. "The building must be strong and safe for people to use. The basement shouldn't leak. And the rooms shouldn't get too hot from summer sunlight streaming in the windows."

But the planning isn't all practical. There is real artistry involved. As Arlene says with a grin, "Architects don't see a staircase just as a way of going up and down. They talk about things like rhythm and direction and pacing of the stairs. They even think carefully about the views from the stairs."

It can take many hours to come up with the final plans. "It's an incredible challenge," Arlene comments. "My goal is to create a space that has all the structural and mechanical details right but is also really pleasing and beautiful."

Supervising

Once the clients have approved the plans, they often want the architect to supervise the project. This means Arlene contacts the local authorities to arrange for permission to build. She instructs the firms to do the construction. She checks the job site regularly to make sure the work is done properly. And she is a go-between for her clients and the construction workers whenever decisions have to be made.

The great moment is the day the project is completed. "It doesn't matter how big or small the project is," smiles Arlene. "There's always a real thrill in seeing your vision become a reality."

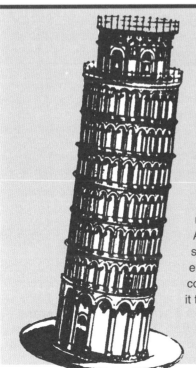

Firm foundations

There are lots of things for architects to consider when designing a new building. A major concern is the firmness of the ground underneath.

One of the world's best known buildings owes its fame to a sandy foundation. The Leaning Tower of Pisa was built on unstable ground more than 600 years ago. And it has been slowly sinking on one side ever since. In the early 1990s, engineers poured huge quantities of concrete under the tower in an effort to stop it from one day falling over completely.

In most areas there are strict rules about how buildings are constructed. Here Arlene consults these rules, known as "building control regulations".

All in a day's work

Arlene usually has several different projects on the go. But if a job is small, she can get a lot of planning done in one day.

Arlene has just received the approval to design an extension to a two-storey house. "The clients want to expand the kitchen and make a family room on the ground floor," she explains. "Upstairs, they want to enlarge the master bedroom and add a smaller bedroom."

Measuring up

But before anything can be done, Arlene needs to have a set of precise drawings of the house. "Sometimes, if you're really lucky, there are existing drawings. But usually you have to go out and measure the site yourself," she says cheerfully.

Arlene reaches the home by 9 a.m. First, she photographs the house on all four sides. Then she checks the outside dimensions using an extra-long tape measure. Accuracy is important. "This is a brick house, so I'll record the dimensions of two bricks with the mortar in between. That's a trick for when I'm back in the office. If I think there's an error, I can count the number of bricks in the photograph and re-calculate the measurements in that way."

It's a draw

Arlene returns to the office by noon, ready to draw exact plans for the house. She could use a computer, but she decides against it. "The computer is great when you're drawing a large project like a whole block of flats. Then you've got a typical unit that's repeated many times," she remarks. "But for small jobs, I prefer to do the work by hand."

First she chooses a scale: for this project 1 to 50 seems best. Then she draws exact "floor plans". It's like taking the roof off and looking down from above," Arlene explains. "You draw the top floor plan and then lift it off to see the next floor below."

"Sectional elevation" drawings are done next. These are the side views. "Imagine taking the outside walls off a doll's house, one at a time," suggests Arlene. "Then you see all the different floors, one on top of the other."

Imagination at work

Once she has the drawings, Arlene puts heavy tracing paper over the top. Then she's free to sketch some of the ideas she has for changing the space.

Of course, Arlene has been playing with different ideas all day. "While I'm measuring, there are always things at the back of my mind. I imagine how it would be to punch through the wall with doors that open onto a patio. Or I think about turning the staircase in a different direction to make a larger area where people can gather easily."

Sometimes it's a struggle to make the ideas work. The dimensions might not work. Or the change might be too costly. And if the phone keeps ringing with calls from consultants and clients about other projects, it can be hard to concentrate. But this project works like a jigsaw puzzle: the pieces all seem to fall together perfectly.

Arlene leaves the office at 7 p.m., sure that she's found the ideal solution for her clients.

This is an elevation drawing for a fire station renovation project that was designed and supervised by Arlene and her partner, David Eckler. Large-scale projects like this one require massive organization. Covered walkways must be built to protect pedestrians. Traffic needs to be diverted to bring in heavy equipment.

Detail of a floor plan for the fire station restoration showing staircases and toilets.

Which window?

An architect may decide to put in a window. But that's just the beginning. What kind of window should it be? Should it be a rectangle, a circle, or some other shape? Should it be a fixed pane of glass that just lets the light in? Or should people be able to open it?

Here are four different types of opening window.

Which types of window are used in your home? In your school? Why do you think each type was selected?

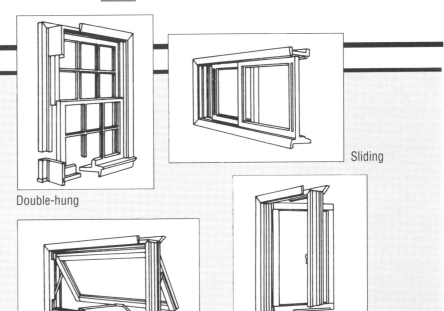

Double-hung

Sliding

Awning

Casement

Activity

Re-model your school library

Think about the way the space in your school library is arranged. How could it be improved to suit you and the people who work there? To test your ideas, you should make detailed floor plans of the way it is now.

You will need
a long measuring tape
a note pad
sharp pencils
a good rubber
a ruler
graph paper
tracing paper

Procedure
1. Measure the space as accurately as possible. Record the measurements as a rough sketch in your note pad.
2. Choose a scale for your floor plan. It should be small enough for the space to fit comfortably onto a single sheet of graph paper.
3. Draw an exact floor plan. Mark in all doors, windows, heating units and fixtures like water fountains and sinks. Allow for the thickness of walls. Indicate which way doors swing open.
4. Now put tracing paper on top of your finished plans and let your imagination go. Move windows and doors. Enlarge work areas. Add curved walls. Consider the location of book shelves, electrical sockets, study tables, computers and the loans desk. Do whatever you think would help to improve the space.

As you plan, try to take into account everyone who uses the library. Will it accommodate wheelchairs? Does the librarian have enough room to work?
5. Show your plans to your librarian and ask for comments. Architects want to know how well the user of a space likes it.

A good architect can make all the difference in how a space works. These offices overlook a central, glass-covered piaza.

How to become an architect

Like many people, Arlene didn't know exactly what she wanted to do when she finished school. It was the courses in art history that helped make up her mind.

Arlene decided to take a degree in architecture. The work was often very practical. "For one course," Arlene recalls, "we were given three months to design a library. At the same time, we studied real libraries that had been built by famous architects. And we also toured local libraries to find out what worked and what didn't."

Practical experience

But getting her degree in architecture was just the first step. "After you graduate, you are required to work for an architect as a kind of apprentice," explains Arlene. "You need to gain experience doing all aspects of an architect's job — drawing, designing, and overseeing a project. At the end of a year, your supervisor signs documents that prove you have spent a set number of hours doing these different tasks."

Arlene has almost finished this practical experience. But there are more hurdles ahead. Trainee architects study for a further two years to obtain a diploma or higher degree, then work for an architect for another year before taking the final exams.

Is this career for you?

"Architecture can be very exciting and creative," says Arlene. "But you have to remember that what you are designing is not for yourself." Successful architects have to be flexible and ready to work with what their clients want. "Of course," Arlene smiles, "you can gently lead your clients. You try to persuade them that a particular way is the best route to take."

Arlene discusses plans for a kitchen renovation with a client. "You've got to find out what the client's needs are and how much money they want to spend," explains Arlene.

An architect also has to be diplomatic in dealing with the workers on a project. Clients often change their minds in the middle of a job and want to add new features. It's up to the architect to keep tempers cool as new schedules and costs are negotiated.

"Being an architect is a real responsibility," comments Arlene. "People put their trust in you to plan a structure that's both strong and appealing. And if there are problems with the final building, such as a leaky roof, you could find yourself being taken to court." This rarely happens, but architects do carry insurance to protect themselves in such cases.

Despite the responsibilities and the long years of education, most architects do not make large sums of money. The rewards are much more personal. As Arlene says, "Nothing can beat the satisfaction when a client turns to you with a smile and says 'Yes, you're right'."

Career planning

Making Career Connections

Ask permission to "job shadow" an architect for a day. Take pictures and make notes of the various tasks done. Think about how you might do these jobs.

Visit a building site and ask to speak to the project manager. Explain your career interests and ask permission to look at the plans for the building or to have a tour of the site.

From your school careers adviser, obtain course calendars for schools that offer degrees in architecture. If you have access to the Internet, you may be able to find this information online.

Ask your librarian to help you find the name and address of the professional association for architects. Write a letter requesting information about membership requirements.

Getting started

Interested in being an architect? Here's what you can do now.
1. Be curious about buildings. When you see unusual staircases or entrances or other architectural features, draw them. Your sketches don't have to be perfect. Just use them to help you sharpen your eye. Keep your sketches together in a folder.
2. Study maths, especially geometry and trigonometry. But you should also study history and art to understand the creative side of architecture.
3. Consider how the furniture is arranged in your bedroom. Could it be organized to make the space more useful?
4. Pay attention to how doors work. Measure the various doors you pass through. Notice which way they swing.
5. Practise drawing simple floor plans using a computer software program.

Related careers

Here are some related careers you may want to look into.
Builder
Follows plans to construct new spaces. Employs carpenters, electricians, plumbers, masons and other tradespeople.
Architectural technician
Makes technical plans for a project showing the construction details, such as where the pipes should run for plumbing.
Interior designer/decorator
Works with clients to select colours, finishes and furnishings for a space. Employs workers to complete the decoration work.
Landscape architect
Designs outdoor spaces. Suggests changes in the shape and slope of the ground. Advises on the use of plants, trees, ponds, fountains, pathways and seating areas.
Building inspector
Works for local government to ensure building regulations are followed.

Future watch

In the recent past, architects have competed to create the biggest, most original, most glamorous buildings. But now the trend is to less flashy projects. Architects are focusing on the three Rs — renovation, restoration, and re-modelling. Their main goals are to make buildings pleasant and easy for people to live and work in.

Stephen Fakiyesi

Fine Artist

PERSONAL PROFILE

Career: Fine artist. "You influence the way people see the world around them."

Interests: "I played five years of school football. But I'm mostly involved in my community and church activities."

Latest accomplishment: "Right now I'm planning an art exhibition with several other artists. I'm the chief organizer and I'll be writing the catalogue for the exhibition."

Why I do what I do: "Art for me is a labour of love. It's also a way for me to communicate how I feel about the society I live in."

I am: "Very concerned and passionate about my community."

What I wanted to be when I was at school: "I wanted to be an architect, or perhaps a doctor. I never considered being an artist. But later I realized it was the career that would make me happiest, even if I didn't earn much money doing it."

What a fine artist does

What comes to your mind when you hear the words "fine art"? Some people imagine formal art galleries where the visitors speak in low, serious voices. Others think of art auctions where thousands of dollars can be spent on a single painting. But for fine artist Stephen Fakiyesi, "Art is more than just a pretty picture on a wall, and it's a lot more than just money."

In fact, "fine art" means any work of art — a painting, a drawing, an object — that is created for its own sake. Some fine artists want to show viewers a new way of looking at nature. Others want to show a new way of looking at the human body. And still others, like Stephen, aim to create images that say something about how society works. As Stephen explains, "I use my art to talk about the situations around me."

Stephen doesn't need an elaborate studio. Instead, he works wherever he can find the space.

The artist's technique

As well as having something to say, fine artists also need the techniques to get their ideas across. Stephen himself has very practical tastes. "I'm not a consumer of too many things," he says thoughtfully. As a result, many of his works are paintings on large sheets of paper. He uses markers, inks, or "any paint that's easily available."

Paper may be fragile, but Stephen doesn't treat it with special care. "When I'm using large sheets of paper, I carry them around, and they crease. So even the creases become part of my work," he explains. Often he will tear the paper deliberately to suit the image he is creating. "In fact, if it's not ripped or torn, you're pretty lucky, with my work," Stephen laughs.

The artist's audience

Like most fine artists, Stephen wants his voice to be heard. For this reason, he displays his art in public exhibitions. Sometimes these shows are sponsored by art galleries or public institutions like schools. At other times, he arranges them himself.

"No matter who organizes the show, Stephen is concerned about how his art will be accepted. Of course the most positive reaction comes when viewers decide to buy a work. And his works do sell.

However, Stephen mainly wants his works to make people think. In fact, in past shows, his art has raised a great deal of passion. It has been loudly praised by some viewers and furiously criticized by others. Both responses are fine with Stephen. "I want people to react strongly to my work. I like to raise important issues."

This picture was created using plywood, paper and five colours of ink. "This is a woodblock print," explains Stephen. "First, I drew the image on a sheet of plywood. Then, I added the colours one at a time. Each time I applied a new colour, I pressed the paper onto the plywood. I had to be very careful that the paper was in the exact same place every time."

All in a *life's* work

For most fine artists, there is no typical day. In fact, as Stephen explains, "Being a fine artist is a whole way of life. It's definitely not a 9-to-5 job." The actual process of making the art is quite intense. It is also very solitary: almost nobody sees Stephen's work until he is ready to have an exhibition.

Hanging the show

Stephen holds exhibitions in many different spaces — galleries, shop windows, even a cafeteria. "I like to show my work where many people will see it, especially those who would not think of going to a normal art gallery."

The day that Stephen hangs a show is a hectic one. For no matter where a show is held, the artist supervises how the works are hung. "It's pretty crazy," he laughs. "I'm trying to get things together right up to the last minute. For the last show,

I even finished one piece the night before I had to hang it."

Once he has the work assembled, Stephen thinks about where each work of art will look best. The spaces are not always ideal. "I did one show where my pictures were hung outside in a public square. I covered the art with plastic to protect it from the rain," Stephen reports. "The plastic became part of the art work itself."

Indoor spaces can also pose problems. "In the space where I had

"Most of my works are very large," reports Stephen. "I made this piece in two sections. The larger-than-life figures were printed on paper and attached to netting. Then, I hung the netting in front of a golden image of a youth with his hands clasped behind his head."

my last show," Stephen says ruefully, "there was an orange wall right in the centre. I didn't know what to do with it at first. I wanted to paint the floor orange or the wall white. But the owners didn't want that, so I couldn't."

Stephen removes masking tape from a partly finished outdoor mural.

Ahead of their time

Many famous artists had a rough reception from art critics when they first showed their pictures.

Look at this landscape by A. Y. Jackson. When this artist and his contemporaries first exhibited in 1920, one critic dubbed their paintings "hot mush". Others complained that the pictures were far too daring and "avant-garde". Today, the group's works hang in galleries, museums and private collections around the world. What is your reaction to this landscape? How do you feel about today's modern art?

Waiting for reactions

Once the works are hung, Stephen waits for the opening of the show. Just like a singer, actor or dancer before a performance, he feels a rush of energy and nervousness. Questions race in his head. How will the audience react? Will they like his work? Will they want to buy it? And, more important, will they understand what he is trying to say?

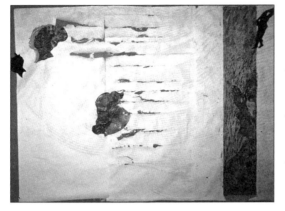

"The gallery owners were really worried about hanging this piece, called *Worship*," laughs Stephen. "They were afraid they'd damage it. I'm not as careful as they would be. Because most of my work isn't framed, I usually just lay it face down on the floor and tape the entire back of it. Then I tape the piece directly to the wall. I go through a lot of tape."

Activity

Create your own paper

Like most painters, Stephen is particular about the surfaces he uses. Sometimes commercially made paper just doesn't seem right. "On a trip to Nigeria," he reports. "I saw a lot of hand-drawn advertisements there that really inspired me." To re-create the effect of these signs, Stephen made his own paper from discarded newspapers and magazines. In this activity you can try your hand at producing your own sign paper.

You will need
- old newspapers
- water
- a bucket
- white glue
- an empty round plastic bottle, such as used for shampoo
- a piece of screening in a frame
- a sheet of plastic, such as a green bin bag
- four empty soup cans (washed carefully)

These are a few of the signs Stephen created for a recent exhibition at his local community art space.

Procedure
1. Shred several sheets of newspaper into small strips.

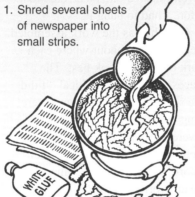

2. Place the shredded paper in the bucket. Add as much water as the paper will absorb. The mixture should be very mushy. Leave it for an hour or so until the paper strips have begun to fall apart.

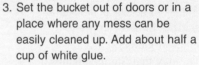

3. Set the bucket out of doors or in a place where any mess can be easily cleaned up. Add about half a cup of white glue.
4. Using the empty plastic bottle, pound the mixture in the bucket. Keep pounding until the mixture is quite smooth. This could take as long as 30 or 40 minutes.
5. Take several handfuls of the mixture and spread it onto the screen. Roll the paper flat with the empty bottle, allowing the excess water to drip away.

6. Using the soup cans, prop the screen and paper over the plastic sheet, and leave it to dry for a day or so.

Once your paper is dry, try your hand at drawing on it with markers. How does the texture of the paper affect the look of your image?

How to become a fine artist

For students who have completed school, there are many different art courses available.

As Stephen explains, "It's possible to become a fine artist without going to college. But courses can be really helpful." For one thing, they give students an opportunity to experiment with different techniques. They also introduce students to key people in the art world. "But most of all, art courses teach you how to look critically at your own work."

Showing their work to the public is vital for artists. Some artists join co-operatives, renting studio and display space as a group. Others sign an "exclusive contract" with a gallery owner promising to give the owner up to 50% of all sales.

Whatever arrangements the artist makes, it is important to learn some business skills. The most secure fine artists are those who have learned to market their works to the public.

Distinctive style

Every fine artist develops an individual style. Often the style is so personal that experts can tell who created a work just by looking at it. The way the paint is applied, the use of colour, the arrangement of the objects, and the contrast between light and shadow are all important parts of an artist's style.

Examine these two landscapes. Each one shows sky, trees, water and buildings. But they are painted in very different styles. How would you describe the differences in style between the two artists?

Ronciglione by Garth Speight

Rustic Landscape by Wayland

It's a Fact

Not all fine artists are appreciated during their lifetime. Vincent Van Gogh (1853-1890) painted nearly 600 pictures, but he died a poor man. In fact, he sold only one painting in his lifetime. Not long after he died, collectors began to pay attention to Van Gogh's works. Their value has increased dramatically: on the 100th anniversary of his death, one of Van Gogh's portraits was sold for more than $82 million.

Is this career for you?

Have people told you that you have artistic talent? Do you find it easier to express yourself in images than in words? If so, the career of a fine artist might be for you.

But to be a fine artist requires more than talent and technical ability. It requires a whole different attitude to life itself. Fine artists are people who are willing to make enormous sacrifices to pursue their visions and dreams.

It is possible to make money from fine art, but very few artists manage to live on what they earn from selling their work. They depend on grants from government or private agencies. Or they take on commercial jobs, like Johnny Gibson (see page 22). Or they take temporary jobs to provide themselves with food and shelter. For example, Stephen does odd jobs, ranging from teaching art to children, to selling encyclopedias door to door.

On the other hand, being a fine artist can be enormously fulfilling. As Stephen remarks, "Success, to me, is having the opportunity of doing what I love to do. Money and security aren't so important."

Career planning

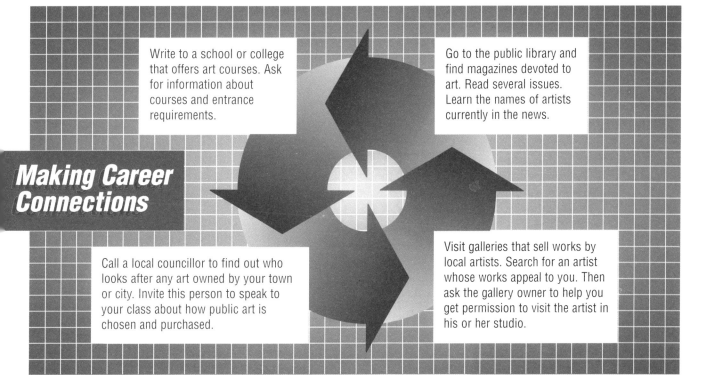

Write to a school or college that offers art courses. Ask for information about courses and entrance requirements.

Go to the public library and find magazines devoted to art. Read several issues. Learn the names of artists currently in the news.

Making Career Connections

Call a local councillor to find out who looks after any art owned by your town or city. Invite this person to speak to your class about how public art is chosen and purchased.

Visit galleries that sell works by local artists. Search for an artist whose works appeal to you. Then ask the gallery owner to help you get permission to visit the artist in his or her studio.

Getting started

Interested in being a fine artist? Here's what you can do now.
1. Study art and art history.
2. Compare several paintings, or sculptures, or other art works to see the different techniques artists use.
3. Practise making art. Respond to a book you have read. Express your reaction to a football game.
4. Experiment with inexpensive materials like pencil, chalk, spray paint and plasticine.
5. Go to an art supply shop. Ask about different supplies available.
6. Be in touch with the world around you. Have something to say about what you read, see and hear in the news.
7. Read reviews by art critics. If possible, attend the art shows yourself and decide whether or not you agree with the critics.

Related careers

Here are some related careers you may want to look into.
Curator
Works in an art gallery. Advises on art purchases. Organizes exhibitions and writes descriptions of the works on display.
Art dealer
Buys and sells works of art. Advises clients on art purchases. Often represents several artists.
Critic
Writes summaries and criticisms of art shows and events for the media. Discusses new trends in art.
Art historian
Studies the development of art over the years and in various cultures. Lectures and writes books on art and artists.
Performance artist
Mixes art and drama to make a statement about the world. Creates a work of art in front of an audience using words, gestures and various objects.

Future watch

Artists are, by definition, creative people who look at the world in different ways. While there will always be room for artists working with traditional materials, many others are expanding their techniques. In the future, more and more artists will mix new technologies, such as computers and lasers, with traditional methods of expression.

Deanna Glen — Industrial Designer

What do the words "industrial design" mean to you? Most people react the way Deanna Glen did when she first heard the term. "I thought of nuts and bolts and grease and big warehouses," she recalls with a grin. "But it's not that at all. In fact, I really think it should be called product design."

Deanna has a good point. Industrial designers are concerned with any product that is manufactured: from car bumpers to cots, from lamp posts to washing machines, from telephones to televisions. They are the

professionals in between the engineers and the customers. As Deanna explains, "The engineer knows whether or not a product can be built and the best materials to make it from. The designer makes sure the product looks right and feels right.

Deanna researched, designed and personally built this prototype, or model, for a mobile garden trolley. There are hooks for tools, a waste bin and plenty of room for pots and bags of soil. All the moving parts on the cart are bright yellow to set them off from the fixed parts which are grey.

Pioneering design

What do the soft drink dispenser at a fast-food restaurant and the passenger cabin of the Concorde jet have in common? They were both designed by one person, Raymond Loewy. Loewy worked as an engineer, fashion illustrator and window display designer. He pioneered the profession of industrial design in the 1920s. The design firm he started is now one of the largest in the world.

Training

When she left school, Deanna knew she wanted to do something creative, so she took a foundation course at an art college. There, she learned about courses available in industrial design. "At my college," explains Deanna, "there was an emphasis on practical experience and working with manufacturers in the area. But some colleges require a much heavier maths and science background because their courses are engineering based." Whatever their emphasis, these courses all require at least three years of study.

Some industrial design students land full-time jobs right after graduation. But many, like Deanna, begin by working on short-term projects for different companies. "I really like the flexibility of contract work," says Deanna enthusiastically. "I can't imagine myself settling down yet to a steady job. That can come later."

Getting started

1. Make plasticine models of everyday products.
2. Put together a product for which some assembly is required. Rewrite the directions to make the task easier.
3. Test the different pens for sale at an office supply shop. Which pen has the best design?
4. What changes would you make in your classroom to accommodate someone who was very tall? A person in a wheelchair? Sketch your designs, or make a model.

Stephen Muirhead — Graphic Designer

When Stephen Muirhead shops at a chemist or supermarket, chances are he'll come face to face with his own creations. That's because Stephen, a graphic designer, spends his days designing packages. He sees his work on everything from sweets to detergent, from toothpaste to lipstick.

Stephen didn't always dream of this career. In fact, in high school he intended to be a police officer. The turning point came when he wrote an essay for an economics course. "My paper was pretty bad," he laughs. "I spent most of my time designing a fancy cover. I got a C for the essay. But my teacher gave me an A+ for the cover and said that I should consider going into graphic arts!"

Stephen rarely talks directly with clients. Instead, he talks with his firm's marketing representatives. These reps are "go-betweens". They convince clients to use the firm's services. They also make sure the designers understand exactly what the clients want. "The marketing reps take all the heat if the clients aren't satisfied," Stephen grins. "I'm happy to avoid the politics."

It was a wise suggestion. "As a kid," recalls Stephen, "I spent most of my time doodling and drawing cartoons." He had just never thought of turning his doodles into a career.

After school, Stephen entered a three-year course for graphic artists. But the early parts were heavy on theory. So he left and went to another college where the courses were more practical. "Some people like to follow rules. But I'm happier figuring things out as I work along," he explains.

Graphic revolution

Stephen has been employed by the same firm since he graduated. And in that time he has witnessed a whole revolution in graphic design. He was off for two years because of injuries he suffered in a motorcycle accident. "When I left, we were doing the work by hand on drawing boards. When I came back, we had fax machines and computers. Now, I never use the drawing board."

When he goes into work each day, Stephen can never be sure what project the office manager will assign him. He may work on a coupon, or seminar materials, or a sales flyer. The project might be brand new, or one that's almost complete. As Stephen explains, "Often you may come up with a design. But by the time it actually gets printed it's been changed by lots of different people."

There's no room for ego in graphic design. It's a team effort that gets the job done. The artists behind the packaging are always anonymous. But Stephen doesn't need personal fame. He gets satisfaction from doing his best.

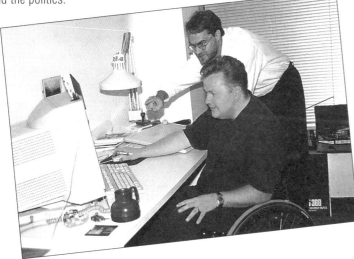

Getting started

1. Pay attention to magazine and newspaper advertisements. Draw the ads that you really like and play around with them.
2. Copy your favourite comic book figures. Draw them doing different actions.
3. Create an original T-shirt design and have it printed.
4. Examine the packaging on the products you buy. How are the print and pictures arranged?
5. Produce the programme for a school event.

Christine Arnet — Stained Glass Artist

Have you ever admired a stained glass window, or enjoyed the glow from a stained glass lamp? Whether it was made 100 years ago, or just last week, you can be sure that the item was cut and assembled by hand, one piece at a time. The techniques used by modern stained glass artists like Christine Arnet have hardly changed in hundreds of years.

An accidental career

Christine never planned to have a career in stained glass. Instead, she wanted to illustrate children's books. "After school, I studied illustration and design," she recalls. "But it's really hard to get started in book illustrating, so I took on whatever jobs I could. Just by chance, one job was for a woman who owned a stained glass studio."

Christine was first employed to enlarge a sketch to make a life-size pattern for a window. But the owner also needed a helper to cut out the glass for a complicated lamp. "She put a pair of cutters and a pair of pliers in my hands and showed me how it was done," laughs

Christine. "There were about 3000 pieces in that lamp. It took me nearly a month to cut them all. That was more than seven years ago, and I've been in the business ever since."

Christine stands at the light table where she does much of her work. The window on the table and the glass window leaning against the wall were both designed by Christine. The lamp hanging from the ceiling was made by her partner. Choose any one of these items and count how many individual pieces of glass you can see.

Painstaking work

As Christine discovered, all stained glass articles must be assembled with great care and patience. For one thing, the work can be dangerous. "You cut yourself just about every day," laments Christine. "You can easily burn yourself as you're soldering the metal that holds the pieces of glass together. And you sometimes need to treat the glass with toxic chemicals."

These days, Christine is part owner of her own studio. It is now her turn to employ helpers. She also helps a steady stream of customers. They may want to buy ornaments on display, have windows repaired, or ask Christine to design a new window made specially for them.

With all these interruptions, Christine can never judge exactly how many hours it takes her to make an article. If a piece seems to take her longer than she expected, it doesn't trouble her too much. "Stained glass is very addictive," she smiles cheerfully. "It's a wonderful career."

When glass and water mix

Washing windows regularly is a good idea. It helps prevent damage caused by weather and pollution. But under certain conditions, water actually damages glass. Some modern glass can deteriorate in just a few days if it is kept moist and warm. If sheets of wet glass are packed tightly together, they will soon bond permanently into a single large block.

Getting started

1. Study art and design.
2. Visit buildings where you can see stained glass windows. Observe carefully how these windows are constructed.
3. Research the different types of glass: cathedral, opalescent, mouth blown, flash and ripple.
4. Buy a kit from a craft shop and make your own stained glass article.

Sheldon Parks — Antiques Shop Owner

By the time he was seven, Sheldon Parks was already on the way to becoming an antiques dealer. He loved to poke around antiques shops on Saturday afternoons, asking questions about the age, origin, use, and value of the objects for sale. "I'd ask about the furniture, silver, porcelain — any item that caught my eye," recalls Sheldon with a laugh. "Once the owners realized I wasn't going to buy anything, they'd tell me to come back with my parents and chase me out."

It was a superb education. "Everybody thinks that just because something is an antique, that it must be rare," explains Sheldon. "In fact, you keep seeing the same things repeatedly. I would listen to what one dealer said about a particular porcelain vase, for example. Then, when I saw the same vase in another shop, I'd ask again. I also

remembered and compared their prices. Eventually it became a kind of game for me to identify things."

As he grew older, Sheldon no longer pestered shop owners. Instead, he started working for them part time in the summer holidays. After school, he gained a degree in art history and museum studies.

"It was good training, to a point," he says, "but you only really get to know the objects by working with them."

In business

His opportunity came when he landed his first full-time job working for an auction house. Sheldon's main responsibility was to appraise the porcelain and glass items to be sold. That meant writing detailed descriptions of the size, style, age and condition of each item. It also meant suggesting a price for each. Sheldon could make good guesses by finding out the price of similar items sold in the past. But there are always surprises in the world of antiques. No one can predict for sure what a customer might be willing to pay.

These days, Sheldon is in business for himself. He travels widely, arranging the sale of peoples' household goods, searching out treasures and buying and selling porcelain, furniture and jewellery. "It's a fantastic life," he says enthusiastically. "I spend my time with beautiful objects. I do become attached to some things. But I also know that I'm just babysitting them for the next owner. We all are."

Dealers are always on the alert for forgeries and fakes. The red mark on the base of this vase says that it was made around 1720. But Sheldon's practised eye immediately tells him the real date is more like 1970. He knows this from the brown colour of the gold decoration and from the way the flower pattern was applied.

Getting started

1. Visit antiques shops and ask questions about the objects. Read books on the decorative arts. Learn about the different periods and styles. Make a game of memorizing makers' names and marks.
3. Go to auctions. Compare the final sale prices to the ones suggested in the sale catalogue.
4. Study art and history. Focus on the furniture or decorative styles that were popular at different times.

Classified Advertising

Help Wanted

DTP OPERATOR Advertising co urgently requires flexible adaptable individual with design skills to look after their network, hardware & software. Knowledge of Quark, Photoshop & Illustrator essential. Fax CV to 324 4990

FINANCIAL ASSISTANT needed. The successful applicant must have 3-4 years' all round bookkeeping/accounts prep exp, strong communication and team work skills, good PC/spreadsheet skills and a previous medium/large sized company background (ie Top 500 plcs). Salary negotiable. Phone Steve, 488 8931

Newsline Group – Online Sub-Editors
Successful applicants will be part of a team whose responsibilities include the electro... the internet. You ... computer literate and ... enthusiastic about ... new online publish... Internet...

PHYSIOTHERAPIST

Plumchester Community Health Centre is seeking a part-time physiotherapist. The centre offers a multidisciplinary approach with special focus on Senior Education and Health Promotion. A competitive salary and excellent benefits are offered. Candidates must be fully qualified with at least two years' experience and eligible for registration with the Society of Physiotherapists.

All applications to be received by 4 June. Please send CV to the **Personnel Manager, Community Health Centre, 30 Norman Road, Plumchester.**

MARKETING COORDINATOR
Prestigious independent computer user association seeks a dynamic individual to help market its membership services and events. Marketing degree and ...perience desirable; self-motivation ...al. Some travel involved. Salary ... CV to: PYC, Adele Bedfo... Thyme Street, Bigley-by-Sea, PH...

TRAINEE MAN...
Limited positions... ...bitious individuals to work... specialist team of a high profile and... ...ic private company. Full training... potential for ...ior management an... ...it share, ...table for experience... ...ates and ...fessionals.
...further details, pleas... ...Clarke on 351 3129.

MANAGER
Environment... Services

We are seeking a bright, ... motivated professional with broad understanding of ...onmental issues to assist ... development and c... ...ation of comp...
policies and progr...
new const...
managemer...
regions of...
governmer...
Please...
for interv...
Road, P...

Admin...tion

The Marb...on Hote... well educ...and well individual... ...oin them... Administ... Departmen... establish... working prac... role requi... ...etermined a... numerate... ...iduals, with ... Custome... ...ice skills, wh... coordinate... ...t Office billi... thoroughly... ...tigate invoic... If you fulfi... ...quirements, a... prepared to... ...shifts, have s... previous exp... ...ce within a H... Reservations... ...ption or an... Accounting e... ...ent and are... seeking a fresh... ...enge, please... CV with a han... ...covering le... to:

Stanley Weber,...
Personnel and ... ...g Mana...
The Marbellington...
Plumchester, PH2 ...

Shop Assistant Needed

Treasure House Antiques requires a shop assistant to work at weekends. Duties include sales transactions, gift wrapping, organizing displays, answering the phone and delivering small parcels. The successful applicant will have proven to be a reliable, responsible worker, able to deal tactfully with the general public. Sixth-form students preferred. Personal references required. Interested applicants should apply in person, with curriculum vitae, to:

Mrs Lucy Meanwell
Treasure House Antiques
32 Baskerville Road
Plumchester
PH7 6BZ

...mmunity Law...rs
...ies)
...t an employment sp...ism ...Unit. You will work... ...a ...hone consultancy... ...ling ...housing special... Both ...ill supervise t...se by ...r work in th... ...owing ...Employm... At least ...essent... ...Rose, ...nchester

...rs to work on KPT ...ssful applicants will have ...iversity degree and a nose for news. KPT also needs a Sales Executive to market KPT information products to the media and those interested in the media's diary. The successful applicant will have a university degree, knowledge... ...ence of dealing with inf... ...ducts. Salary +... ...onnel Manager, ...use, 14-17 Green Street, ...umchester, PH3 4DG.

...m, **Redhill Lane, Plumchester.**

Snap...t Processing
...require an

Analytical Laboratory Technician
...r the QC Dept. Candidate must have experience in Wet Analytical Techniques (Potentiometric and UV Determinations). Post involves chemical mixing and weekend work. Applicants must be qualified to a minimum of 'A' level in Chemistry.
Apply in writing with CV to: Mr Swift, 26 St Barnabas Road, Greater Bigley. PH3 4GN.

Medical Statistics... Computing Statistician

A statistician is required ... ...istance in the Department's teaching, research a... ...candidate will be required to provide advice to undergraduate medical students and health professionals, analyse data using SPSS or SAS, assist in teaching to professions allied to medicine, and provide support for the installation and usage of statistical and related software packages. An MSc in medical statistics preferred. Familiarity with statistical packages and a good level of computing ability and communication skills are essential. Salary according to experience.

Applicants should send a full CV to the **Personnel Department, University of Plumchester, Plumchester, PH4 5RT.**

East Plumchester Clinical Audit Department
Clinical Audit Facilitator
The Clinical Audit Department measures and critically appraises the work of East Plumchester Community Healthcare Trusts. The ideal candidate will have a degree in the behavioural sciences, be computer literate and familiar with statistical packages (SPSS). He or she will also have excellent data analysis and communication skills. For an application form please contact the Personnel Department, Whitchurch Hospital, Whitchurch High Street, Plumchester PH2 3HZ. Tel. 355 648. Please quote ref CA/EP/346.
Working Towards Equal Opportunities: Plumchester Healthcare

Who got the job?

Finding a job

The first step to success in any career is getting a job. But how do you go about finding one?

- In the field of art and design, many jobs are advertised by word of mouth. Talk with family, friends, neighbours and teachers and let them know what jobs interest you.

- Respond to "Help Wanted" ads in newspapers.

- Post an advertisement of your skills on a community notice board.

- Contact potential employers by phone or in person. Volunteer your services if no paying jobs are immediately available.

- Send speculative letters to companies and follow up with phone calls.

A job application usually consists of a letter and a curriculum vitae (CV – a summary of your experience and qualifications for the job). Applicants whose CVs show they are qualified may be invited to a job interview.

Activity

Recruiting a shop assistant

The advertisement shown on the opposite page, for a part-time job as a shop assistant in an antiques shop, was placed in a local newspaper. This is a chance for anyone interested in art and design to spend time working with decorative objects. It offers an excellent opportunity to train your eye, while you learn about different artistic styles and periods.

The ad tells applicants to go directly to the store, taking a CV with them. When applicants submit their CVs directly to Mrs Meanwell, they should be prepared to be interviewed briefly on the spot. The first impression they make will determine whether or not they have a serious chance at the job.

For the position of shop assistant, there might be many applicants. Two of the applicants were Anita Marchant and Desmond Wong. Their letters and CVs and the notes made by Mrs Meanwell during the interviews, are shown on pages 46 and 47.

Procedure

Make a list of the qualifications that you think are important for a good assistant in an antiques shop. Now consider each applicant's CV, covering letter and performance during the job interview. Which candidate has the best qualifications and experience? What else, besides qualification and experience, did you consider in making your decision?

Challenge

How would you perform at a job interview? Role-play an interview in which a friend plays the part of Mrs Meanwell. Then reverse roles. Role-playing will give you practice in asking and answering questions. This practice can help make sure that when you apply for a job, you have a good chance of getting it.

Anita Marchant's application and interview

6 Josephine Road
South Plumchester
PH13 4OH

21 May 19-

Mrs Lucy Meanwell
Treasure House Antiques
32 Baskerville Road
Plumchester
PH7 6BZ

Dear Mrs Meanwell

I would like to apply for the position of shop assistant that was advertised in the Plumchester Chronicle. I have enclosed my CV with this letter.

I have always been interested in art and decorative objects. I have my own collection of spoons from different places I have visited. My parents have several pieces of antique furniture including a pine chest made in the 1880s. I enjoy using and caring for this furniture very much.

Currently I work part-time on Sundays at the coffee shop at the Plumchester Public Library. I take orders, serve food and collect payment. I believe it is important to give cheerful, prompt service. I also feel confident that my experience has been excellent training for working at such a place as the Treasure House.

Working in your shop would give me a wonderful opportunity to learn more about antiques and collecting. I would be very grateful if you were to ask me for an interview. I can be reached by telephone any time after 4 p.m.

Yours sincerely

Anita Marchant

Anita Marchant

Interview: Anita Marchant

- neatly dressed in blouse and plain black trousers
- was enthusiastic about the shop; genuinely appreciated merchandise
- has never broken any items in coffee shop; slipped once on wet floor but managed to save the plates she was carrying
- does the gift wrapping in her family
- once had a customer try to leave without paying; called the manager to handle situation
- needs to give two weeks' notice to coffee shop before could start

Anita Marchant

6 Josephine Road
South Plumchester
PH13 4OH

Age: 16

Education: I will leave Plumchester Sixth Form College next year. I have taken optional courses in history and art.

Employment: I have worked for two years as a server at the Coffee Shop, Plumcheste Public Library. Since I was 13 I have been a pet and house sitter for severa local families when they have been on holiday.

Interests: Reading — I have been an active member of the Plumchester Library since I was 11.
Gymnastics — I have been a member of school gymnastics team for two years. Our team was overall winner of the 19— championship. I won individual second prize on the beam.

References: On request.

Desmond Wong's application and interview

23 May 19–

Mrs Lucy Meanwell
Treasure House Antiques
32 Baskerville Road
Plumchester
PH7 6BZ

Dear Mrs Meanwell
I was very interested to read your ad in this week's Plumchester Chronicle.

I am currently attending my final year at South Bigley College of Technology where I have taken as many art options as possible. My goal is to pursue a career in some area of art and design.

At college, I have worked as a voluntary assistant to the art tutor, designed the posters for student union events, and helped make scenery for the drama club. During the past two summers, I worked for a local playscheme, where I was responsible for the art room for younger children. I planned different projects, set up displays of the children's artwork and spoke regularly with their parents.

I believe my knowledge of art and the responsibilities I have voluntarily taken on have been good preparation for a job in your shop. If you have any further questions, I can be reached by telephone any time after college at the number below. Thank you for your consideration.

Yours sincerely

Desmond Wong

Desmond Wong

Desmond Wong

- *cleanly, neatly dressed*
- *polite and confident manner*
- *felt cash register would be no problem since he's familiar with computers*
- *had some problem with over-eager parents at playscheme, but was able to resolve situations diplomatically*
- *only available for summer; going to art college next September*

Curriculum Vitae – Desmond Wong

"The Groves"
Appleblossom Lane
Bigley-by-Sea

Education
South Bigley College of Technology, 19 — - 19 —
- Finishing final year, taking optional courses in art and computers
- Member, drama club
- Class representative, student union, 19 —

Voluntary Experience
Art Room Assistant, South Bigley College of Technology
- Organized art supply cupboards
- Kept up-to-date inventory of materials
- Helped students working with computer art software in after-school club

Playleader
- Supervised daily, one-hour art sessions for 7-10 year-olds
- Planned projects
- Ordered supplies, staying within set budget

References: On request.

Index

Credits

(l = left; r = right; t = top; b = bottom; c = center; bl = bottom left; br = bottom right)

All illustrations by Warren Clark.

All photographs by David Rising, except 7 (b), 8 Jeanne Capone; 6 (br), 12 (l) (c), 16, 18 (br), 20, 28, 29 (r), 32, 34, 35 (t), 36 (bl), 37 (b), 38 (b), 40 (l), 42, 43 Gillian Bartlett; 17, 18 (bl) Jo Anne Sommers; 18 (tr) Art Gallery of Ontario; 19 Ewa Dziadowiec; 24 (l) (c), 25 (r) Johnny Lee Gibson/David Rising; 30 Arlene Hofstader/David Eckler; 31 (b) Makrimichalos-Cugini Architects; 35 (b), 36 (tr) (br), 37 (t) Stephen Fakiyesi; 38 (t) Garth Speight.

Answer
Page 14: 106 gm or 3.7 ounces